Prepare the Way

Celtic Prayers for the Season of Light

Copyright © Ray Simpson, 2019.

Anamchara Books
Vestal, New York 13850
www.AnamcharaBooks.com

Prayers on pages 52, 74–80, and 85 are adapted from the *Carmina Gadelica*. Prayer on page 46 is from H. S. Coffin's translation of "Come O, Come Emmanuel" (1916), and prayer on page 47 is from T. A. Lacey's 1906 version of the same Latin carol.

Scripture quotations are the publisher's own translations from the original Greek.

IngramSpark 2020 paperback ISBN:
978-1-62524-791-9

Cover and page design by Micaela Grace.

Celtic knotwork by Sergey Abalentsev.
. Cover painting by Joseph Farquharson.

Prepare the Way

Celtic Prayers for the Season of Light

RAY SIMPSON

Contents

Introduction	9
Advent	17
Winter Solstice	43
Christmas Day	61
New Year's	101
Epiphany	115

The voice shouts out of the emptiness, prepare the way of the Life Giver, make God's path straight.

—Mark 1:3

Introduction

The Christmas season is a liminal time, a betwixt-and-between time. It marks the threshold between the eons before and after Christ's emergence into time and space. It is also the season of the winter solstice, when light and dark are equal.

The Celts loved thresholds—the places where water met earth, where light met dark, and where this world and the Otherworld met and mingled. These were sacred times and places—Thin Places, where the Holy could be glimpsed with our physical eyes, where the Presence of God could be sensed with ears and skin, where the very taste of the Divine might linger on the tongue.

These holy thresholds are the containers for paradox, and we find paradox everywhere in the Christmas story: a virgin gives birth; the Divine Infinite is contained within a human baby; the Eternal Word is expressed in the birth cry of an infant; Almighty God becomes helpless and vulnerable; the Creator of all Reality takes the form of one who is poor, rejected, homeless; and the marvelous news of a King's birth is revealed first to shepherds, ordinary working-class people. *The Word became flesh and pitched his tent among us* (John 1:14a, from the Greek). The full expression of the Divine One—the Word—took on the weakness, finiteness, and limitation of human flesh. This paradox is the threshold into a new understanding of Reality.

A paradox is a mystery, something we cannot explain with rational logic. It is a concept that does not yield easily to the linear thinking of the patriarchy; it requires a more inclusive, all-embracing attitude, like that of a mother's love or a child's wonder. But in our scientific age, we are often uncomfortable with the concept of mystery. As Dietrich Bonhoeffer wrote:

> The lack of mystery in our modern life is our downfall and our poverty. . . . We retain the child in us to the extent that we honor the mystery. Therefore, children have open, wide-awake eyes, because they know that they are surrounded by the mystery. They are not yet finished with this world; they still don't know how to struggle along and avoid the mystery, as we do. We destroy the mystery because we sense that here we reach the boundary of our being, because we want to be lord over everything and have it at our disposal, and that's just what we cannot do with the mystery. (*God in the Manger*, page 18)

Mystery requires both humility and wide-awake eyes. Without it, Bonhoeffer cautioned, we know "nothing of the mystery of our own life, nothing of the mystery of another person, nothing of the mystery of the world." We pass over all that is hidden in ourselves and others; we live "on the surface, taking the world seriously only to the extent that it can be calculated and exploited, and not going beyond the world of calculation and exploitation." Without mystery, our lives are impoverished and stunted.

And yet year after year, the Christmas mystery offers itself to us. Wrapped up in tinsel and commercialism, it nevertheless remains unchanged. It brims with the message that God chose to express God-Self not through power or violence or prestige, but through a helpless baby born into a poor family.

"Whoever sees me sees the Father," Jesus told us (John 14.9). If we see God in the Christmas mystery, then our entire understanding of our lives and the world in which we live will be changed, for this is not a mystery confined to the month of December, to the season of lights and evergreen and shopping. This is a mystery that stretches from the birthplace of one Child out into infinity.

John continued his description of the Incarnation with these words: *and we saw his brightness, the splendor of God's only child, the full expression of kindness and grace* (John 1:14b, from the Greek). The beauty of kindness, of gentleness and love, shines forth from the Incarnation. The true nature of God is revealed to us. Saint Peter Chrysologus wrote that the Divine became a child so that we might cease to be afraid of God.

This doesn't mean that we can now forget about God's claim on our lives. Instead, we stand on the threshold of a new intimacy with God. We see the Divine Presence in all things small and vulnerable, in all the people the world has overlooked or rejected, and we embark on a new relationship with the Creator of all life. God can no longer be regarded as

Someone faraway and aloof; now, God is present everywhere we turn, waiting for us to open our hearts to receive the Divine Presence.

When the Celts first encountered the Christmas story, they readily opened their hearts and minds to this tale of mystery and paradox. It embodied the meaning they already celebrated at the time of the Winter Solstice, a time when the Yule log lit the darkness of winter and celebrated the return of the sun's light and warmth, when the holly and ivy symbolized the evergreen life that endured even in cold and darkness. For the Celts, the Christmas season was a "Thin Place," when the Holy Otherworld overlapped our everyday world, filling even the ordinary with extraordinary meaning.

Ray Simpson has given his life, both professionally and personally, to Celtic Christianity, and now he helps us to celebrate a Celtic outlook on the season of Christmas. With their eloquent yet simple words, his prayers welcome the Holy One who comes to us in small, ordinary ways, who is present in the helpless and the vulnerable. As we join Ray in prayer, we stand on the threshold to paradox and mystery—and we "prepare the way" for God to enter our world anew.

—Ellyn Sanna
Anamchara Books

Advent

The radiance that is truth is coming into the universe, to give light to all humanity.

—John 1:9

Calm us to wait for the gift of Christ.
Cleanse us to prepare the way for Christ.
Teach us to contemplate the wonder of Christ.
Anoint us to bear the life of Christ.

In the wasteland may the Glory shine.
In the land of the lost
may the King make his home.

All-knowing God,
parents-in-God picture
and pattern Your ways;
forgive us for following idols and illusions.
All-seeing God, prophets shine
like candles in the night;
forgive us for staying in the dark.
All-holy God, front-runners like John
clear obstacles from Your path;
forgive us for blocking Your way.
All-giving God,
people like Mary offered their all
as bearers of Your life;
help us to be bearers of Your life.

Lord, though we may laugh
at failed end-of-world predictions,
may we live this day
as if You will come
and find us doing our duty with joy,
alert and ready to meet You.

Help us to prepare a way for You:
by our thoughtfulness towards others;
by our care in little things;
by our upholding of the oppressed.

Help us to prepare a way for You:
by our thoughtfulness toward creatures;
by our care of crops and kitchens;
by our upholding of creation.

The earth is becoming a wasteland:
Breath of the Most High, come and renew it.
Humanity is becoming a battleground:
Child of Peace, come and unite it.
Society is becoming a prison:
Key of Destiny, open doors to our true path.
The world is becoming a no-man's land:
God-with-us, come and make Your home here.

Christ, Light of the world,
meet us in our place of darkness.
Christ, Light of the world,
meet us in our place of longing.
Christ, Light of the world,
meet us in our place of working.
Christ, Light of the world,
illumine our darkness.

Among the hungry,
among the homeless,
among the friendless
come to make things new.
Among the powerful,
among the spoilt,
among the crooked
come to make things new.
In halls of fame,
in corridors of power,
in forgotten places,
come to make things new.
With piercing eyes,
with tender touch,
with cleansing love
come to make things new.

Come to us, Wisdom,
moving in the flux and flow of the cosmos
to bring worlds into being.
Come to us, Wisdom,
permeating all creation,
the life of soil and seed and seasons.
Come to us, Wisdom,
shaping nations and ensouling peoples.
Come to us, Wisdom,
encompassing the mysteries
of the unseen world
and the mysteries of the soul.

Come to us, Wisdom,
the seeing eye of art and science,
the ear of all that breathes.
Come to us, Wisdom,
the light of our darkness,
the reconciler of that which is divided.
Come to us, Wisdom,
the weaver of Earth's destiny,
the completer of our call.

Wisdom, permeating creation and
informing all peoples,
come and bring us the mind of God.
Shaper of peoples,
who through Moses gave guidance
that would make a people great,
guide us into the ways of true greatness.
Bedrock, Sign of community,
come to places of instability
and root them in realities
that nothing can destroy.
Key to Destiny, unlock our potential
and our capacity to befriend and serve others,
that we may be mentors and soul friends
amid a needy people.

Light-Bringer,
illumine places of
darkness, despair, and disease.
True Fulfiller of Desire,
harness our deepest longings
to Your infinite purpose of love
God-with-Us—
the Presence that cannot be taken from us—
may we live with You
and may You live in us forever.

Great Spirit, swirling in the elements,
You brought to birth a world.
Mighty Creator, swirling in the elements,
You brought to birth a Son.
Eternal Christ, swirling in the elements,
You stride towards us now.
Glory to God in the highest.

You are holy, You are whole.
Let Earth give praise from pole to pole.
You are coming, coming here
to bring Your hard-pressed people cheer;
bringing to them human birth
born of heaven, born of earth;
bringing to them bread and wine,
giving hope of life divine.
You are coming, You are whole.
Let Earth give praise from pole to pole.

Desire of every nation,
we bring to You those who are empty
and who long to find meaning.
Come to them, Lord Jesus.
Desire of every nation,
we being to You those who are overlooked,
who long to know their worth.
Come to them, Lord Jesus.
Desire of every nation,
we bring to You those who are exploring,
but who do not know what they search for.
Come to them, Lord Jesus.

Lord, You keep us waiting for signs of hope.
You keep us looking for ways
in which You come.
The pain of the world,
the anguish of the people
cry out to You.
Come, Lord Jesus, come.

Child of the prophets, on our longings
let Your light shine.
Child of Mary, on our littleness
let Your light shine.
Child of Eternity, on our lying down
let Your light shine.

We wait in the darkness,
expectantly, longingly;
come, O God Most High.
In the darkness we can
see the splendor of the universe—
blankets of stars,
the solitary glowings of the planets.
Come, O God Most High.
In the darkness of the womb
mortals are nurtured
and the Christ Child was made ready
for the journey into light.
Come, O God Most High.
In the darkness the wise three
found the star that led them to You.

Come, O God Most High.
In the darkness of dreams
You spoke to Joseph and the wise ones
and You speak still to us.
Come, O God Most High.
In the darkness of despair and distress
we watch for a sign of hope
from the Light of Lights.
Come, O God Most High.

God be with us on our
journey towards Christmas.
Help us to go deeper into what is real
until we are brought to
the wonder of Your incarnation.
Dear Son of God, You took flesh to redeem us.
Forgive our hardness.
Dear Son of Mary,
with sacrifice of love You came to us.
Forgive our selfishness.

With Abraham and Moses,
waiting to be led to a place of promise,
we wait.
With Amos and Hosea, Isaiah and Micah,
and all the prophets believing that
You are a God of justice,
we wait.
With Paul and Silas,
and all God's people
imprisoned and persecuted,
we wait.
With Naaman and Jairus,
Bartimaeus and the Syro-Phoenician woman,
longing for an end to pain and rejection,
we wait.

With Zaccheus in his tree
and the Samaritan widow at the well,
keen to be liberated from a half-life,
we wait.
With Sarah and Hannah, Elizabeth and Mary,
looking forward to new life
and new beginnings,
we wait.
With Jesus in the desert,
and in the garden because he asks us to,
we wait.

God of time and eternity,
prepare our minds to celebrate with faith
the commemoration of Your birth on earth.
Fill our hearts with joy and wonder
as we recall the precious moment
when You were born as our brother.

May we journey with You,
Jesus, Mary and Joseph,
to Your birthplace at Bethlehem,
firm in the faith,
loyal to the truth,
obedient to Your Father's will
along the path that leads to life.

Winter Solstice

*The Light
illuminates the darkness,
and the darkness
does not grab hold of it.*

—John 1:5

Lord of the solstice,
on this day of briefest light,
help us to be at home
with the treasures of the dark.
As the days have drawn in
help us to flow with the ebb tides of life.
At the turning of the year
help us to welcome the Dawn from on high.

We arise today
in the simplicity of the empty soil,
in the strength of the fierce elements,
in the deep formation of winter.
Stripped of inessentials we stand,
rooted in You.
In the anticipation of gathering strength,
You sustain our well-being.
In the humility of the bare earth
we invite You to do Your work in us.

Christ at the yearly turning,
Christ at every bend.
Christ at each beginning,
Christ at every end.
Christ in dark's deep shadows,
Christ in shades of death.
Christ in primeval history,
Christ in wintry earth.

At this time of briefest light,
may we bunker down with You,
grateful for memories, storing riches,
finding well-being in winter's patterns.

In the chill of wintry wind,
in the depths of uncertain thoughts,
sing to us the story of the universe,
visit us as Savior of our being.

Star Kindler and Weaver of Wonder,
as winter stars light up the darkness of night,
reveal to us fresh sources of hope.

Hold us, O God of the cold, dark days,
secure in the knowledge
that from its wintry depths
the earth brings forth a Savior.

Creator God,
whose power and beauty are never spent,
in wintry earth waken us
to the mystery of Your presence.

Creating and Sustaining God,
as this cold, dark season encroaches,
give to us the stability of the deep earth
and the hope of heaven.

We arise today
in the deep formation of winter,
in the transforming power of ice,
in the cleansing work of frost.
We arise today
in the simplicity of the bare earth,
in the strength of the fierce elements,
in the beauty and brilliance of snow.

Stripped of inessentials we stand,
rooted in You.
In the anticipation of gathering strength
You sustain our well-being.
In the stillness of the bare earth
we invite You to do Your work in us.

Thank You for leading us
to the time of briefest light
secure in the trust that
You embrace the encircling gloom,
held by the dark which
You encompass in Your arms,
content to rest in
You like a baby in the womb.

We bind to ourselves this day
    the strength of rock,
    the silence of earth,
    the sharpness of cold.
We bind to ourselves this day
    the longevity of stars,
    the integrity of sky,
    the sobering of dark.

Counsellor, quicken our souls' progress
in this winter season.
Kindle in our hearts fires of
welcome and love,
in the presence of the Holy Trinity,
in the presence of the angels without envy,
in the presence of the saints without fear.

When cold night draws near
we draw near to You.
When dark cares loom large
we draw near to You.
In our hard place of need
we draw near to You.

The world is not dead,
it is sleeping.
Its life draws in,
it is keeping.
The earth is gathering energy
for a new burst of life.
We breathe in the mystic air
that we may breathe out care.
Your presence supports us through the night
so we can hail the coming source of Light.
Shine through the mists,
the deadening heavy clod,
gladdening Light of Christ our Lord.

Lord of the seasons,
on this day of briefest light
help us to be at home
with the treasures of the dark.
As the days have drawn in,
draw near to us with Your everlasting light.
As shadows lengthen,
help us to embrace the shadow side of life.
As the dark swallows up the created sun,
help us to store up riches
for the long days ahead

God of time,
God of dark,
God of earth,
God of heaven,
You are
stronger than the elements,
stronger than the shadows,
stronger than the fears,
stronger than human wills,
stronger than the spirits,
stronger than magic spells.

Your presence be our shield.
The love of God to enfold us,
the peace of God to still us,
the Spirit of God to fill us,
the saints of God to inspire us,
the angels of God to guard us
this night, this winter, forever.

Christmas Day

*Glory to God
in the highest Heaven
and on Earth
wholeness and harmony
to humanity,
God's delight.*

—Luke 2:14

O come, Thou Wisdom from on high,
who orders all things mightily;
to us the path of knowledge show,
and teach us in her ways to go.
Rejoice! Rejoice! Emmanuel
shall come again and with us ever dwell.

O come, Desire of nations, bind
all peoples in one heart and mind;
bid envy, strife and quarrels cease;
fill the whole world with heaven's peace.
Rejoice! Rejoice! Emmanuel
Shall come to thee, O Israel.

O come, O come, thou Dayspring bright!
Pour on our souls thy healing light;
Dispel the long night's lingering gloom,
And pierce the shadows of the tomb.
Rejoice! Rejoice! Emmanuel
Shall come to thee, O Israel.

O Come, thou Lord of David's Key!
The royal door fling wide and free;
Safeguard for us the heavenward road,
And bar the way to death's abode.
Rejoice! Rejoice! Emmanuel
Shall come to thee, O Israel.

Jesus, born in a stable,
make here Your home.
Jesus, born of a peasant girl,
make here Your home.
Jesus, searched for by wise seekers,
make here Your home.
Jesus, reared at a carpenter's bench,
make here Your home.
Jesus, risen from the wintry ground of death,
make here Your home.

Universal Child,
we will welcome You when You call.
We open the long-shut parts of our lives.
We will become young again with You.

O Christ,
You entered the stream of human life:
immerse us in the divine life.
Immerse us in the waters that cleanse.
Immerse us in the waters
that overwhelm evil.
Immerse us in the waters of creativity.
Immerse us in the waters of life everlasting.

Dearest Christ,
the earth gave You a cave,
the skies gave You a star,
the angels gave You a song
and we give You our love.

Thank You for the Holy Family,
Mary, Joseph, and the others.
May families reflect Your love;
may purity, love, and trust
grow strong in our households.

This night is the eve of the great Nativity,
Born is the Son of Mary the Virgin,
The soles of His feet have reached the earth,
The Son of glory down from on high,
Heaven and earth glowed to Him,
All hail! let there be joy!

The peace of earth to Him,
the joy of heaven to Him,
Behold His feet have reached the world;
The homage of a King be His,
the welcome of a Lamb be His,
King all victorious, Lamb all glorious,
Earth and ocean illumed to Him,
All hail! let there be joy!

The mountains glowed to Him,
the plains glowed to Him,
the voice of the waves with the song of the strand,
announcing to us that Christ is born,
Child of the King of kings
from the land of salvation;
shone the sun on the mountains high to Him,
All hail! let there be joy!

Shone to Him the Earth and sphere together,
God the Lord has opened a Door;
Son of Mary Virgin, hurry now to help me,
You, Christ of hope, You, Door of joy,
Golden Sun of hill and mountain,
All hail! let there be joy!

Infant Jesus,
truly God, truly human,
truly infinite, truly frail,
Your greatness holds the universe;
Your face attracts our hearts;
Your goodness beckons all that is good in us;
Your wisdom searches us;
Your truth reshapes us;
Your generosity enriches our poverty;
Your hand fills us with blessings;
Your mercy brings forgiveness.
Your glory fills the world.

Babe of heaven, defenseless Love,
You had to travel far from Your home.
Strengthen us on our pilgrimage
of trust on earth.
King of glory, You accepted such humbling;
clothe us with the garments of humility.
Your birth shows us the simplicity
of the Creator's love;
keep us in the simplicity of that love.
Your coming shows us
the wonder of being human;
help us to cherish every human life.

Christmas Day

Christ, splendor of the Father's glory,
sustaining all the worlds
by Your Word of power,
renew Your presence in our lives.
Christ, child of Mary, rich in wisdom,
Prince of Peace, God with us,
renew Your presence in our homes.
Christ, begotten of the Father before time,
born at Bethlehem in time,
renew Your presence in Your Church.
Christ, truly God, truly human,
fulfilling the desires of the peoples,
renew Your presence in the people.

God of time,
God of dark,
God of earth,
God of heaven,
You are
stronger than the elements,
stronger than the shadows,
stronger than the fears,
stronger than human wills,
stronger than the spirits,
stronger than magic spells.

Christmas Day

Your presence be our shield.
The love of God to enfold us,
the peace of God to still us,
the Spirit of God to fill us,
the saints of God to inspire us,
the angels of God to guard us
this night, this winter, forever.

Thank You for the prophetess Anna
who, honed in daily attunement to You
in the offering of praise,
discerned Your presence in an ordinary
but significant moment.
Take our senses, hone our intuition,
steep us in the disciplines of the Spirit,
that we may see Your hand at work
in the events of today and tomorrow.

Thank You for the sanctuaries of Egypt
that were offered to the Holy Family,
for their acquaintance with God-honorers
of another land and religion,
for the hermits and holy people of the deserts.
We pray for God-honorers
who seek to welcome Your servants
in Egypt, in Muslim lands, and everywhere;
for refugees, for hermits
and others who pattern
an alternative way
to that of our acquisitive society.

Thank You for the home in Nazareth,
and for the boy Jesus
growing in skills of carpentry
and in the confidence of puberty.
We pray for young people who are confused,
unskilled, orphaned,
and who know
neither themselves nor their calling:
may they find affirming adults
to be alongside them.

Thank You that even at the death of Jesus
the Holy Family grew
through the adoption of John
into Mary's family.
We pray for those who have died,
and for those who face loss
of life or limb or hope.
May the healing light of Christ
shine upon them,
and may they come to know that there is
a family more wonderful
than they have ever known.

Lord of time and eternity,
prepare our minds to celebrate with faith
Your birth on earth.
Fill our hearts with wonder
as we recall the precious moment
when You were born as our brother.

May every lone parent and child
be cherished as Mary cherished You.
May those who are out in the cold
find a stable place as warm as Yours.
May those who work on the land
be as responsive to Your presence
as were the shepherds.

Let the cares of the past grow dim
Let the skies and our hearts grow clear
Until the Son of God
comes striding towards us
Walking on this earth.

Jesus, proclaimed by angels;
    light up our darkness
Jesus, worshipped by shepherds;
    light up our darkness
Jesus, adored by wise men;
    light up our darkness
Jesus, God who is with us now.
    Light up our darkness.

Jesus, You are the glory of eternity
shining among us,
the tenderness of God here with us now.
Jesus, You are the Healing Person,
the pattern of goodness,
fulfilling among us the highest human hopes.
Jesus, You are the champion of the weak,
the counsellor of the despairing,
the brother of us all,
who knows our every need.
Jesus, You are the splendor of the Father,
the Son of Mary,
our Bridge between earth
and the world beyond.

Angels' Lord, who for nine months
was hidden in love's furnace, Mary's womb,
You who stole down to earth,
humbler than all–
Take us to Yourself, and make us like You.

The love that Mary gave her Son
may we give to the world;
the love that You give us through Your Son
may we give back to You.

Son of the elements, Son of the heavens,
Son of the moon, Son of the sun,
Son of Mary of the God-mind
Son of God, first-born of all creation
dwell with us today.

Child of glory, Child of Mary,
born in a stable, King of all,
Your greatness holds the universe.
You came to our wasteland,
in our place suffered.
Draw near to us who to You call.
Bless to us this day of joy.
Open to us heaven's generous gates.
Strengthen our hope.
Revive our tired souls
till we sing the joys of Your glory
with all the angels of heaven.
Hold also
those who are sleeping rough,
those who feel shut out of society,
those who are cold and hungry
and these we name before You now.

Bless, O Lord, this Christmas tree,
all that goes on to it
and all that goes on around it.
May the needles that point upward
lead us to worship the Creator
who came from heaven to be born as a child.
May the needles that fall to the ground
remind us of the needs of the poor
and those at the bottom of the social pile.
May the decorations that brighten
this dark season
prompt us to celebrate it
with thoughtfulness and joy.

Child of Glory, Child of Mary,
at Your birth You were proclaimed
the Prince of Peace.
You came to remove the wall
that divides one people from another;
may walls of hostility and fear
come tumbling down

Today, O Lord,
as we contemplate Mary and Joseph,
may we live in the wonder
of Your divine conceiving;
may we live in the wonder
of our divine receiving.

O Savior Christ,
You existed before the world began.
You came to save us and we are witnesses of
Your goodness.
You became a tiny child in a cot
showing us the simplicity of our Parents' love.
You chose Mary as Your mother
and raised all motherhood
to a divine vocation.
May all mothers be bearers of life and grace
to their husbands, their children
and to all who come to
their home.

Child of glory, Child of Mary,
born in the stable,
King of all,
You came to our wasteland,
in our place suffered
Come to us now with Your call.

Birther, Father, Mother of the cosmos,
breathing through all creation,
breathing Your life through a woman's womb
into a human form:
bring new birth to us who gather
at this time of the Birth.
Bring birth to our nation,
to this ailing, ageing world,
and bring to birth in us,
who are Your people,
the new creation
which we stand on tip-toe to see.

Hey the Gift, ho the Gift,
Hey the Gift of the living.
The fair Mary went down upon her knee,
It was the King of glory
who was on her breast.
To tell to us that Christ is born,
The King of kings of the land of salvation.
I see the hills, I see the strand,
I see the host upon the wing.
I see angels on clouds, waves
coming with speech and friendship to us.
The world is alive with good news,
telling us that Christ is born.

Hey the Gift, ho the Gift,
Hey the Gift of the living.
Child of the dawn, Child of the clouds,
Child of the planet, Child of the star,
Child of the rain, Child of the dew,
Child of the Milky Way, Child of the sky,
Child of the flame, Child of the light,
Child of the sphere, Child of the globe,
Child of the elements, Child of the heavens,
Child of the moon, Child of the sun,
Child of Mary of the God-mind,
And the Child of God first of all news.
Hey the Gift, ho the Gift,
Hey the Gift of the living.

I AM the Gift, I am the Poor,
I AM the Human of this night.
I AM the Child of God in the door,
Child of the moon, Child of the sun
Great Son of Mary of God-like mind.
A cross on each right shoulder,
I am in the door, open to Me.

See the Virgin approaching,
Christ so young on her breast.
O Mary Virgin! and O Holy Son!
Bless the house and all therein,
bless the food, bless the cupboard,
bless all we keep within our house.

When food is scarce,
It is you, Virgin, who is a mother to us.
You are brighter than the waxing moon
rising over the mountains.
You are brighter than the summer sun,
under his fullness of joy.
You bore Jesus into our world,
the Baby of Heaven, the Baby of Love,
the Child who brings us peace.

The night the star shone
was born the Shepherd of the Flock,
of the Mary Mother.
The Trinity eternal was by her side,
in the manger cold and lowly.
So come now and give what you can
to the Healing Man.
The foam-white Baby beloved,
without one home in the world,
the tender holy Baby rejected and homeless.
Immanuel! God with us!

You three angels of power,
Come you, come you down;
greet the Christ of the people.
Kiss His hands,
dry His feet
with the hair of your heads;
and O! world-pervading God,
and You, Jesus
and Michael and Mary,
do not forsake us.
Stay with us this Christmas morn.

Blessed the King,
without beginning, without ending,
to everlasting, to eternity,
every generation for aye,
ho! hi! let there be joy!

New Year's

*Forget the things that used to be.
Stop analyzing the past.
Look! I am making something new.
It is sprouting into life now.*

—Isaiah 43:18–19

In this new year,
let us foster respect for each person
because God's image is in them.
Let us seek to relate to that
which is of God in everyone.
Let us listen for divine harmonies,
develop friendly creativity
in our communities,
protect Nature, and bring back wonder
into science, learning,
and even in mundane jobs.
Let us foster inspired leadership in business,
politics and media,
starting with ourselves.

God bless to us this year,
never vouchsafed to us before.
It is to bless Your own presence
that You have given us this moment, O Lord.

Bless to us our eyes
and everything they shall see.
Bless to us our neighbors;
may our neighbors be a blessing to us.

Bless to us our households
and all our dear ones.
bless to us our work
and all that belongs to our provision.

Give to us clean hearts
that we may not need to hide from You
one moment of this new year.

God, bless to me the new day,
Never vouchsafed to me before.
It is to bless Your own presence
You have given me this time, O God.
Bless my eye,
and may my eye bless all it sees;
I will bless my neighbor,
and may my neighbor bless me.

Lord of the years,
we will ring out the old year,
the lust to gain,
the craze to destroy,
we will ring in the new year,
the joy of being,
the will to transform

God of the years,
at the gate of the year we put our hands in Yours.
As the old tide recedes,
may we plant Your footsteps in fresh sands.
May we travel with
less baggage and more wisdom.
and learn from You how our journey should be.

Lord of the year behind us,
Lord of the year before us,
as Mary and Joseph
named Jesus in the temple,
may we name Him in our hearts,
receive Him in this Eucharist
and journey with Him through this year.

Bless to us this time of threshold,
when we pass from the old to the new.
Bless to us this bread,
made from grains of wheat that pass away,
that it may become for us
the food that nurtures new life.
Bless to us this wine,
made from grapes that pass away,
that it may become for us
the drink of heaven's ever-renewing life.

Lord, with joy and for love of You
we commit ourselves to seek and do
Your perfect will in this coming year.
We are no longer our own but Yours.
Put us to what You will;
place us with whom You will;
let us be put to work for You
or put aside for You;
let us be full, let us be empty;
let us have all things, let us have nothing.
We freely and with all our heart
give You all things for You to use.
May we walk with You through this year
in unity with our fellow Christians,
feeding upon Your word,
honoring all people,
serving our neighbor,
responsive to the leading of Your Holy Spirit.

You have given Your all to us.
May this food and drink of angels
fortify us to give our all to You
in all whom we shall meet
and in all that we shall do
throughout the coming year.

Holy Father, Holy Jesus, Holy Guide,
be a smooth way before You,
a guiding star above You,
a keen eye behind You;
this day, this year, for ever.

Epiphany

*For the earth will be drenched
with knowledge
of the abundance and glory
of the Living One.*

—Habakkuk 2:14

We welcome Your light
that glints in the rising sun.
We welcome the light
that dawns through Your only Son.
We welcome Your light
that gleams through growing earth.
We welcome the light
that You kindle in our souls.

As once You changed water into wine
change our drear day into sweet rest in You.
Change the drudgery of the old and worn
and of all for whom life's sparkle has gone.

The magi searched for an infant king;
Christ, lead us into Your presence.
They offered incense as their prayer;
Christ, we bow in awe before You.
Myrrh they gave to mourn Your death;
Christ, to You we pour out our suffering love.

Purify our lives like gold
that we may be royal priests to You.
Sanctify our hearts like incense
that we may be adorers of Your presence.
Beautify our hearts like myrrh
that we may be Your fragrance on earth.

May Your presence
draw people across the world
and reveal Your mother heart of compassion.
Pour into the empty cups of the world
the beauty and blessings of Christ
and gather together Your children.

You who became poor to make many rich:
transform our dullness with radiant light;
transform our drabness with vibrant joy.
Transform our shallowness
with deepening wisdom;
transform our suffering with growing trust.

About the Author

RAY SIMPSON is a founding guardian of the international Community of Aidan and Hilda. In 2016 he moved from the Holy Island of Lindisfarne, UK, where the Community has a base for resources, study, and retreat, to a new Community House in Berwick-Upon-Tweed on the nearby mainland. Ray is the author of numerous bestselling books on Celtic spirituality, including *The Celtic Book of Days: Wisdom from the Ancient Saints for Each Day of the Year* and *Celtic Christianity: Deep Roots for a Modern Faith.*

THE WORK OF CHRISTMAS
The 12 Days of Christmas with Howard Thurman

This book is a celebration of the twelve days of Christmas, offering us a chance to dwell on the meaning of the season in dialogue with the wisdom of one of America's greatest mystics and activists, Howard Thurman.

During the twelve days of Christmas, our goal is to experience God's light, despite the temptation to close our hearts in a world too often characterized by racism, sexism, polarization, nationalism, and exclusion. This season asks us instead to open our hearts and our lives, so that throughout the year ahead, we may be light-bearers, carrying the message of Divine justice and hope, making it come alive even in the darkest corners of the world. This is the year-round work of Christmas!

Paperback Price: $10.99

Kindle Price: $5.99

I WONDER AS I WANDER
The 12 Days of Christmas with Madeleine L'Engle

How can we recover the radical meaning of the Christmas season? Using the thoughts and words of Madeleine L'Engle, this books offers you a guide through the hectic Christmas season. In the twelve days of Christmas, bookended by Christmas Eve and the Feast of Epiphany, you will experience anew the awe and wonder of the Incarnation. As you both wonder and wander, the questions and images in this book will open your heart to the radical message of Christmas. Like the Magi, you too can follow a star, seeking wisdom in everyday life, while contemplating the cosmic forces within which we live and move and have our being.

Paperback Price: $10.99

Kindle Price: $5.99

THIN PLACES EVERYWHERE
The 12 Days of Christmas with Celtic Christianity

Bruce Epperly invites you to share a Christmas adventure with him, voyaging through the 12 days of Christmas (plus Christmas Eve and Epiphany) with Brendan, Columba, Brigid, Patrick, and other Celtic saints. With these Celtic adventurers as your companions, you will discover "thin places"—moments of time when the Incarnation of Christ shines through ordinary people, places, and events. After the busyness of Advent, the days that follow Christmas can be a quieter time, when you can venture out on an inner vision quest for new ways of seeing and being.

May your Christmas journey awaken you to thin places everywhere.

Paperback Price: $10.99

Kindle Price: $5.99

SANTA CLAUS
Saint, Shaman, & Symbol

If you don't believe in Santa, you might want to reconsider. The familiar fellow dressed in red has been around a lot longer than the malls' Santa, longer than Rudolph, longer even than "The Night Before Christmas." His earliest and most ancient forms brought hope and cheer to generation after generation of humankind—and he still has a message for us today. In the midst of the materialism of the modern holiday, Santa offers us a bridge between the physical, secular world and the spiritual, sacred realm. Discover his history and evolution, from Ice Age shaman to medieval saint to modern-day icon. Get to know Santa—and believe all over again.

Paperback Price: $12.95

Kindle Price: $5.99

AnamcharaBooks.com

www.ingramcontent.com/pod-product-compliance
Lightning Source LLC
LaVergne TN
LVHW041640060526
838200LV00040B/1653